Workbook:

Increasing Personal Productivity in Healthy and Sustainable Ways

Ursina Teuscher, PhD

Copyright © 2014 Ursina Teuscher
All rights reserved.
ISBN-13: 978-1495300783
ISBN-10: 1495300781

Contents

Introduction 5

The Way Our Brain Works 7
    Temporal Construal Levels 7
    Decision Fatigue 9
    Need for Recovery and Nourishment 11
    Switch Costs 13
    Neuroplasticity 15

What This Mean for Best Practices 17
    Prioritizing and Scheduling 18
        Categorizing Your Tasks 18
        Scheduling Accordingly 23
        Protecting your Priorities 32
    Nourishment and Recovery 33
    Focusing on One Task Only 39
    Forming Habits 43

Trouble Shooting 47
    Frequent Problems 49
        Estimating Time 49
        Following Your Own Plans 50
        Procrastination 53
    DIY Repair: Toolkit For Your Own Assessment and Interventions ... 56
        1. Assessment: Diagnosing the Problem 57
        2. Treatment: Designing an Intervention 64
        3. Rinse and Repeat: Experimenting and Tweaking 67

More About This Topic 84

References 84

Introduction

When it comes to personal productivity, one size does not fit all. Whatever is the best way for your colleague to work, to organize her tasks, and to manage her time may not work at all well for you, and vice versa.

This book takes that into account. It will offer you tools to assess your own work style and situation; it will help you diagnose your own problems and obstacles, and suggest ways to target these problems.

That said, even though we all have different styles and preferences, and our work situations vary greatly, our brains do in fact have a lot of things in common. In order for us to be able to work at our best, it is important to understand some aspects of how our brain works.

Therefore, this book will start out by introducing important findings of neuroscience and psychology. It will then offer suggestions as to how this knowledge can guide your best practices, and how you might apply it to your own work style and situation.

Along the way, you'll find exercises and space to write down your own notes. To get the most out of this book, I recommend reading it with a pen close by, so that you can take those practice opportunities whenever you find them useful.

What made you pick up this workbook?

Give some thought to your current situation.

- What works well?

- What doesn't?

If you could change **one thing** in your work habits, what would it be?

The Way Our Brain Works

What do we know from neuroscience and related research fields about how our brains can work at their best? The answer is: a lot, and many of the findings are very new, since neuroscience is such a recent field of research and has seen incredible advances in just the last few decades.

I believe that of all the research out there, the following topics are particularly important for personal productivity – I will introduce each of them next and explain why:

- Temporal Construal Levels
- Decision Fatigue
- Need for Recovery and Nourishment
- Switch Costs
- Neuroplasticity

Temporal Construal Levels

An interesting framework to have in mind when we are dealing with planning and daily decisions is **temporal construal theory.** It proposes that we think quite differently about events depending on how far in the future they are. When we think about a distant event, we represent it in a more abstract and coherent way, and we connect those future events with our goals. This would be a *high-level construal*. As the event gets closer, we become more concerned about the concrete and incidental details of the events and about the experience itself. This would be a *low-level construal*.

As an example: When I plan to hike next weekend, I'm thinking about the big picture and have goals in mind such as leading a healthy life, making beautiful memories, or enjoying good company.
In the moment of the event itself, from the alarm clock going off at 5:00 a.m. to the strenuous climb and descent, I am likely to focus on the specifics of the experience, including all the discomfort that comes with it. After the event, I will likely look back at it again from the big picture perspective, happy about the memories and achievement.

The fact that we represent future events differently from the present has very practical implications for our decisions: it means that we often make different choices for our future selves than for our present selves. When we're further away from a decision, we find it easy to focus on the big picture and know what's best for us. For example, we know that we want to be productive, eat healthy, work out, and so on. However, as we get closer to the moment when we should actually do those things, we're more likely to choose what feels good in the moment – for example, watch the funny video, eat the chocolate cake, and generally seek instant pleasure and avoid discomfort.

A simple conclusion from this research is that planning ahead of time is a very good idea indeed. Planning can go a long way to help us make choices we won't regret later on, and this book will talk more about how to best plan and schedule below (starting on p. 18). But first, here are some more facts about how our brain works, and how it doesn't (one hint: they will point towards that same conclusion).

Decision Fatigue

Research on repeated decision-making has shown that if people have to make many choices in a row, the quality of their decisions gets worse over time.

For example, one study looked at more than a thousand parole decisions made by experienced judges at an Israeli prison. It turned out that at the beginning of the day, a judge was likely to give a favorable ruling about 65 percent of the time. As the morning wore on, the likelihood of a criminal getting a favorable ruling steadily dropped to zero. After the lunch break, however, the likelihood of a favorable ruling would immediately jump back up to 65 percent. And then, as the hours moved on, the percentage of favorable rulings would fall back down to zero by the end of the day. Regardless of the crime, a prisoner was much more likely to get a favorable response if their parole hearing was scheduled either early in the morning or immediately after a food break, than if it was scheduled near the end of a long session. In other words, the outcome of a decision was highly influenced by how many decisions the judges had already made previously.

Experimental studies have also shown that people are less able to exert self-control after making a series of choices. For example, in one experiment people made choices among consumer goods or college course options, whereas others thought about the same options without making choices. Making choices led to less physical stamina, reduced persistence in the face of failure, more procrastination, and less quality and quantity of arithmetic calculations.
It is noteworthy that choosing seems to be more depleting than merely deliberating and forming preferences about options.

The same pattern was shown for real-life choices as well: researchers asked shoppers in a mall about their experiences in the stores that day and then asked them to solve some simple arithmetic problems. Sure enough, the shoppers who had already made the most decisions in the stores gave up the quickest on the math problems.

Not surprisingly, decisions involving big trade-offs (where both options have considerable positive and negative elements) seem to be the most taxing. However, even unimportant choices, such as between inexpensive gifts, lead to drastically impaired willpower.

Decisions that are especially taxing are those that involve self-control. For example, when people fended off the temptation to eat M&M's or freshly baked chocolate-chip cookies, they were then less able to resist other temptations later on. Willpower really does seem to be a form of mental energy that can be exhausted, which leads us right to the next point.

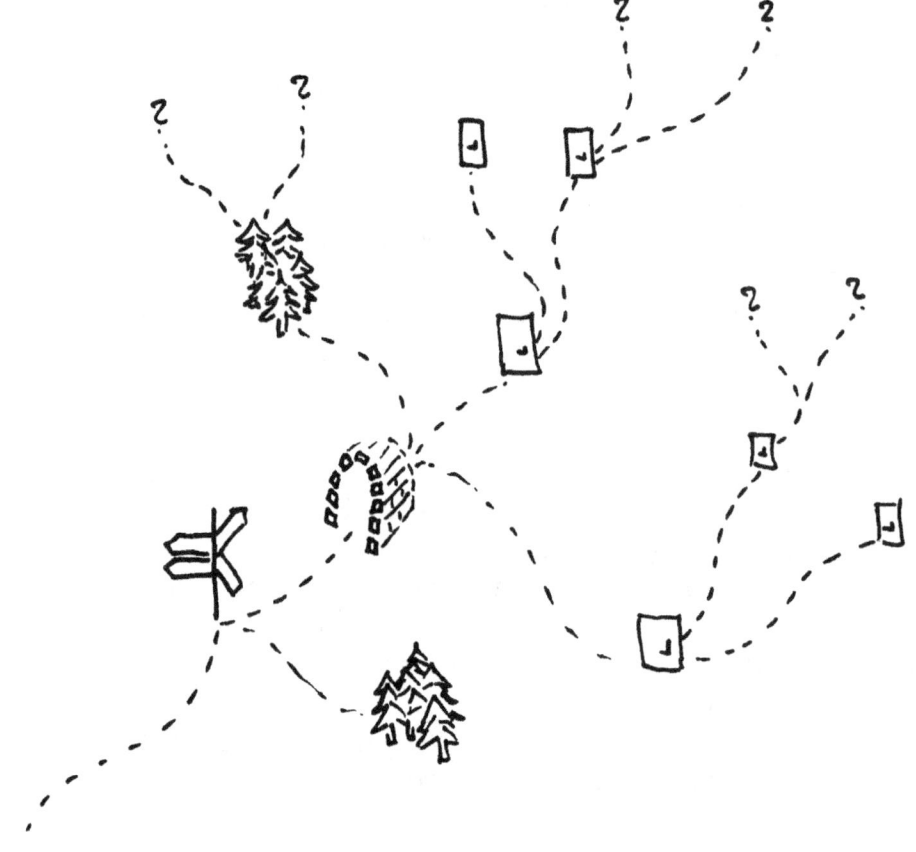

Need for Recovery and Nourishment

Recent research in neuroscience has found that self-control – more so than other kinds of mental tasks – requires a sufficient amount of glucose in the blood.

Low or hypoglycemic levels of glucose seem to lead to impaired decision making, poor planning, and inflexible thinking. In contrast, simple psychomotor abilities, such as responding quickly to certain cues, seem relatively unaffected by glucose levels.

A large number of experiments on different aspects of self-control (e.g., thought suppression, attention control, helping behavior, stifling prejudice during an interracial interaction) have shown the same pattern of findings:

- Acts of self-control reduce blood glucose levels.
- Low levels of blood glucose after a self-control task lead to poorer performance on the next self-control task.
- Consuming a glucose drink after a self-control task counteracts these impairments.
- Sleep and rest also replenish the ability to exert self-control.

In other words, a large body of evidence suggests changes in glucose levels, even subtle or minor changes, can have a profound impact on self-control, and that recovery periods are essential in order to restore our ability make good decisions.

This pattern is in line with other things we know about impulsive behavior and typical self-control problems. For example, research on addiction and criminal behavior suggests self-control failure is most likely during times of the day when glucose is used least effectively, and when people are tired.

We also know, for example, that alcohol reduces glucose throughout the brain and body and likewise impairs many forms of self-control.

Why is self-control so susceptible to glucose? The answer to this question is still controversial. One reason could be that self-control processes are costly and require relatively large amounts of glucose. Processes that require the most glucose might also be the first to be impaired when glucose drops. Another reason could be that when glucose drops, the brain functions that are most central to survival (e.g., breathing, physical coordination) have first dibs on available glucose, not leaving enough for more advanced mental operations.

Both of these ideas are consistent with the general rule that abilities developed last are the first to become impaired when resources are limited. Self-control, planning and decision-making are all processes that involve the frontal areas of the brain – the *pre-frontal cortex,* to be specific. This area is the most recently developed part of our brain in evolutionary history, and it is also the part that takes longest to mature fully in human adolescents and young adults.

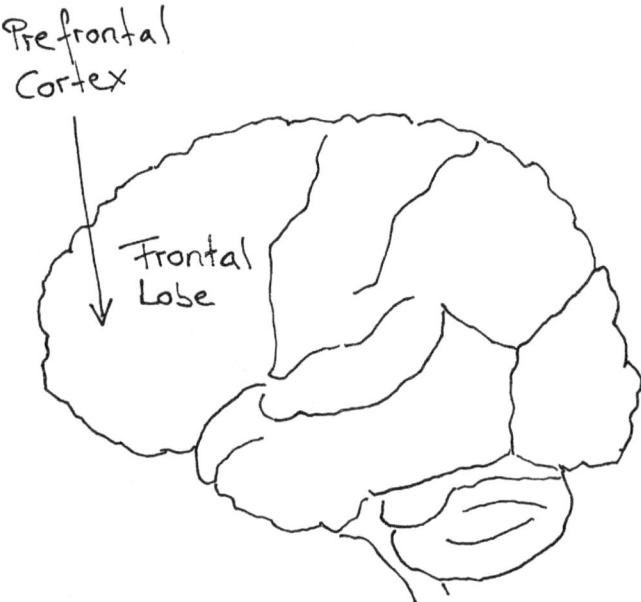

The fact that self-control is so dependent on blood glucose levels and rest has some obvious implications for personal productivity: proper regular nutrition, but also sufficient breaks, rest and sleep, are essential for our thinking, planning and decision-making abilities.

There is also a less obvious conclusion that I draw from this research: since the rest of our abilities are not as easily impaired as our abilities for judgment and decision-making, we may often not realize our impairment. The very capacity (judgment!) that we would need to recognize it is the first one to be impaired.
This means, again, that planning ahead and getting into healthy and regular systems is essential if we want to increase our productivity in the long run, and we will talk a lot more about that below (starting on p. 18).

Switch Costs

Doing more than one task at a time, especially more than one complex task, takes a bigger toll on productivity than most people realize.

An extensive body of research has shown that when people switch between different tasks, their performance on each task is disrupted. The disruption is measurable by slower reaction times and less accurate responses. Neuroimaging studies of task switching have accordingly revealed extra activation in numerous brain regions when subjects prepare to change tasks and when they perform a changed task.

The sketch on the next page shows roughly what extra brain activity is required just for the switching alone. It demonstrates nicely that the switching itself is actually a third task that consumes a lot of brainpower.

The figure also shows that the switch cost occurs in those in frontal areas of the brain that are involved in decision-making and planning – and that are, as we discussed before, very susceptible to fatigue and glucose depletion.

These switch costs are considerable even when people can choose whether and when to switch from one task to another. As tasks get more complex, switching takes an even bigger toll, causing people to lose more time and make more mistakes.

What's more, research on chronic multitasking has surprisingly shown that heavy media multitaskers – rather than being better at multitasking – performed worse on a test of task-switching ability. In particular, they seem to be less able to filter out distracting irrelevant information.

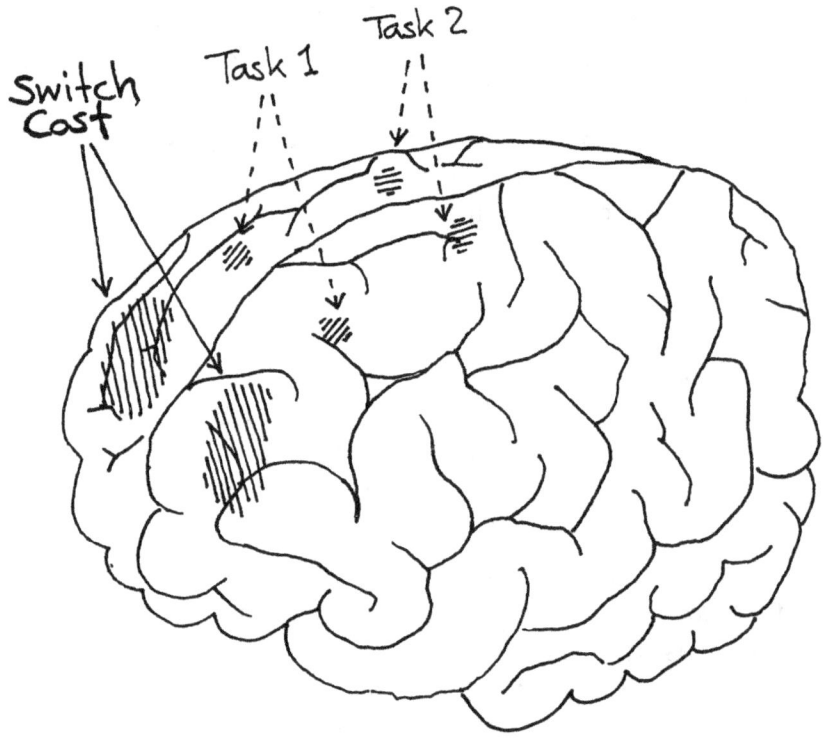

The implications of these findings for personal productivity are very clear, whether we like them or not: we should avoid multitasking by all means. We will discuss later how to best do that in the face of our busy reality (p. 39).

Neuroplasticity

Neuroplasticity is a fancy way of saying that our brains can change.

Early studies on brain development suggested that there were critical periods of development during childhood and adolescence. Neuroscientists used to assume that the neural pathways were more or less fixed after that and stayed the same through our adult lives.
By now though, a large body of research have shown that our brain—even after it is fully developed—does not stop changing. Rather, it appears that our behavior and our experiences keep affecting both the brain's physical structure and its functional organization.

This ability of the brain to change is referred to as *neuroplasticity*.

One of its fundamental principles is that individual connections within the brain are constantly being removed or recreated dependent upon how they are being used.

This idea is captured in the saying:

"Neurons that fire together, wire together".

What this means is that if there are two nearby neurons that often produce an impulse simultaneously, their cortical maps may become one.

This process reduces the overall number of neurons and synapses (also known as synaptic pruning), leaving more efficient configurations.

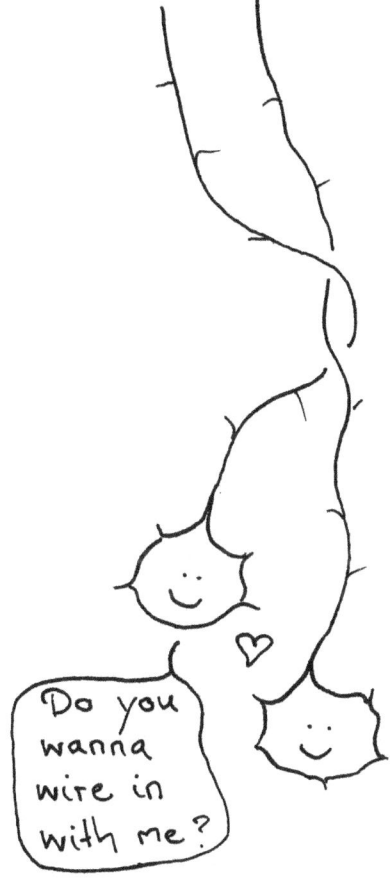

The concept of neuroplasticity is important for our purposes here, because it means that our practices and habits – whatever we do repeatedly, but also the way we think habitually – will have physical effects on our brain. For better or for worse, we can get our brain to rewire, and after practicing certain behaviors, the physical rewiring will make them easier or even automatic.

Luckily, we also know a lot about habit formation, and I will offer some practical guidelines below (p. 43) on how to best form, strengthen and change habits.

What This Mean for Best Practices

Now that we know about all this research, how can we derive best practices from these neurological and psychological findings?

Suggestion:

Before you keep reading, I encourage you to think about the question above by yourself for a moment. You will likely come up with some simple improvements of your unique work situation and habits, simply by thinking about how you could make things easier on your own brain. Whatever you can come up with by yourself – with a fresh mind – will likely be more useful than anything you will read, because you know your own situation best.

I propose the following strategies:

- ❑ Prioritize and schedule *ahead of time*, then follow your own script:
    - To reduce decision-making throughout the day and thereby avoid *decision fatigue*.
    - To take advantage of a *higher-level construal mode*, where you are more likely to make decisions that honor your goals and are good for you in the long term.

- ❑ Take breaks, take time for *nourishment* and *recovery*.

- ❑ *Focus* on only one task at a time to avoid unnecessary *switch costs*.

- ❑ Form good *habits* that will over time become easier or even automatic, thanks to the *plasticity of your neural pathways*.

- ❑ Get good *systems* in place to help with all of the above.

In this chapter you'll find specific tips and exercises for each of these strategies.

Suggestion:

As you read, highlight or take notes of the things you have NOT already been doing (or things you want to try again).

In the end, choose 1-3 things you want to try next.

Prioritizing and Scheduling

Categorizing Your Tasks

Take your to do list, if you have one, or make a quick list of all your tasks you can think of right now. Look at them all and think about how they differ and how they are similar. Becoming more aware of the characteristics of your different tasks will help you schedule them most appropriately. Over the following pages, we'll consider the following dimensions, but you may want to add your own thoughts to those:

1. Urgency vs long-term importance
2. Task demand
3. Location, work setting

1. Urgency vs Long-term Importance

Tasks that appear most urgent are often not the most important ones in the long-term. It takes conscious effort to work towards important long-term goals, rather than on tasks that appear to be urgent, but are in fact less important.

Which of your tasks are most important to you in the long run?

Which will give you the most satisfaction and pride?

Which will likely have a lasting impact on your career or personal fulfillment?

Write all of those down here:

Those are the tasks that deserve prime time in your schedule and require the most protection, because they are likely being pushed off by more urgent—but less important—events.

2. Task demand

Think about the type of cognitive or physical demand a task requires.

Do you have certain tasks that require a lot of *focus*?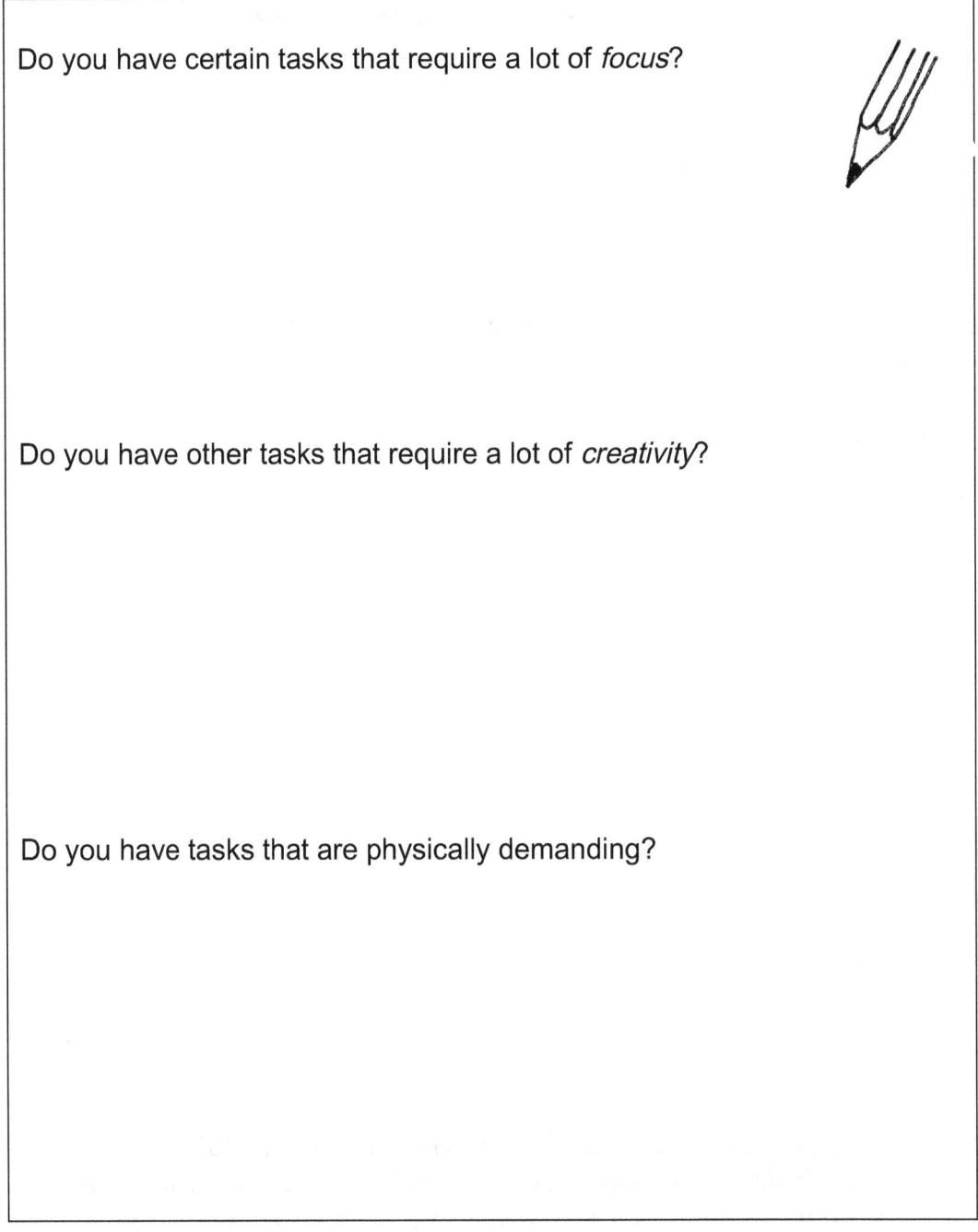

Do you have other tasks that require a lot of *creativity*?

Do you have tasks that are physically demanding?

Research has shown that for most people, *mornings* are best to work on tasks that require *focus*, whereas *evenings* are better for *creative* work.

Also, think about the energy level that your different tasks require.

Are there certain tasks you can still do if you're tired?

Others for which you need to be at your best, physically or mentally?

3. Location, work setting

Determining in what setting you produce your best work (and what tasks can still be done in a not-ideal setting) will also help you schedule.

For example:

- Do you have tasks you do best in your office on your big screen? Other tasks that you do on a tablet?

- Tasks that can be done anywhere? In a coffee shop?

- Tasks for which you need a fast Internet connection? Others than can be done offline?

- Tasks for which you need quiet and privacy?

Write down your own:

Best Work Settings/Locations:	For These Tasks:
•	•
•	•
•	•
•	•

Anything else?

Apart from the three dimensions we covered here (urgency vs importance; task demand; and location/setting), do you have additional differences between your tasks that might matter for scheduling?

Being aware of the characteristics of your various tasks will help you schedule more consciously, which we will talk about next.

Scheduling Accordingly

Next, we will think about what your schedule would ideally look like to best accommodate your different kinds of tasks. How would your perfect day or week be structured?

A good way to schedule is to define "work units" for your tasks. Those units can either be a block of time (e.g., 25 minutes, or 2 hours), or a specific accomplishment (e.g., write one paragraph).

How big those work units should be depends a lot on the type of task as well as on your work style, attention span, and motivation. Different people and different tasks require different units. As a general rule, a task unit should be small enough that you can easily:
        a. get started, and
        b. keep your focus.

Some tasks require a certain warm-up time, after which you may get into a flow. Those tasks obviously require longer time slots where uninterrupted work is possible.

After each of those units, schedule a break. (We'll talk more about breaks below, starting on p. 33). For example, after writing for one hour, take a break. Or, after writing a draft of three paragraphs, take a break. Depending on your tasks, you may not need an actual resting break, but could switch to another activity that is different enough to give you a mental break. For example, you might schedule an hour of focused writing, then respond to emails, and then make some phone calls, and only after that take a break.

Give some thought to your most important tasks right now: what would your ideal *work unit* be for those?
You can think about this either in terms of time (e.g., minutes) or accomplishment (e.g., paragraphs written).

Task 1:

Best work unit:

Task 2:

Best work unit:

Task 3:

Best work unit:

Be Realistic:

When scheduling, it is crucial that we be honest with ourselves as to how much we can realistically get done.

Take into account Hofstadter's Law, and then some:

> *"It always takes longer than you expect, even when you take into account Hofstadter's Law."*

This is also known as the "planning fallacy": individuals as well as organizations tend to underestimate how long it will take to complete a task, even if they're aware of that very tendency.

How can we counteract the planning fallacy and end up finishing our tasks on time? Here are three scheduling tips that can make a big difference:

1. Have mandatory as well as flexible items in your schedule. Treat your most important tasks as appointments, schedule them ahead of time and don't move them around.

2. Have buffers in your schedule — even more than you think you'll need.

3. For important deadlines, set your own deadline earlier than the actual one, but make your fake deadline real by scheduling something fun that you only get to do if you achieve your goal.

What would your perfect day look like, so that you could do all your tasks at the best possible times?

Sketch your ideal schedule on the next pages.

Suggestion:
For this exercise, give yourself the freedom to start with a blank slate. Sketch your ideal schedule with no regards to the current constraints you have.

Version 1 and 2:
You may have different kinds of typical days, for example days that you spend at the office, other days that you spend at home or with clients. If that's the case, sketch different versions of your ideal schedules.
Or, you may prefer to sketch a weekly instead of daily schedule.

Sketch of your ideal schedule (Version 1)

Sketch of your ideal schedule (Version 2)

How far off from this perfect schedule is your real schedule these days? Are there specific constraints that are holding you back from working at your best?

For example, do you have regular meetings in the morning; during the very hours that you would be able to do your best, most focused, work?

Do you have any influence over those constraints? Is there something you can change in your environment (such as talking to your boss?) to make your ideal schedule a reality, or to at least get closer to it?

Write down at least one thing you could do differently to get closer to your ideal schedule.

-

-

-

When to Schedule:

Scheduling ahead of time is essential if you want to take advantage of being in a higher construal level (see p. 7) while you're planning your day. On the other hand, scheduling too far in advance makes it more difficult to be realistic, if a lot is still unknown.

For daily planning, most of my clients benefit if they schedule the night before, rather than on the day itself. It is a nice way to wrap up the day and get ready for next one. The habit of scheduling the day before can make a particularly big difference if you have a hard time getting up and if you are not (yet!) in a regular morning routine that you're happy with.

Similarly for weekly or monthly planning: a regular scheduling routine works best in my experience. For example, put a half hour of scheduling time into your calendar as a repeating event, such as on Friday afternoons for weekly planning, or on the last Sunday evening of each month for monthly planning.

Beware "Binge Working"

"I can't find time to […]"
"I would […] more if I could just find some blocks of time."

By trying to "find" time, rather than schedule it, we end up looking for it during weekends and vacations, when we should be relaxing. If we try to do our most important work during those times, we may easily fall into a vicious cycle of alternating binge working; exhaustion and burnout; inefficiency and procrastination; guilt and stress; more binge working, and so on.

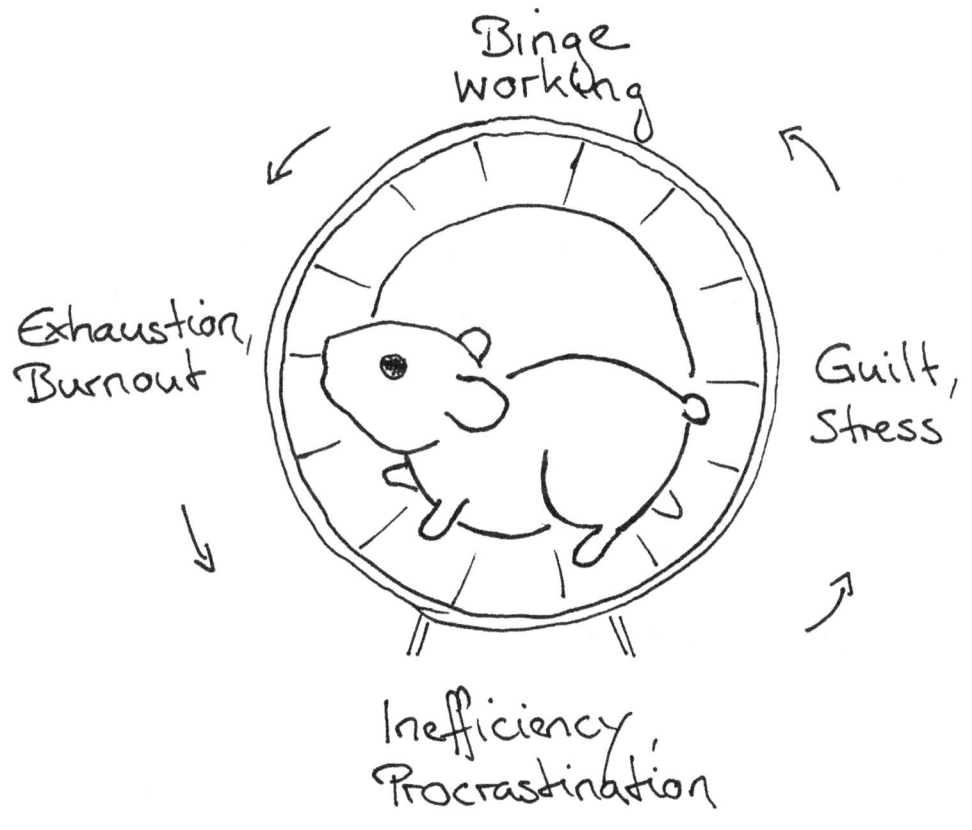

Protecting your Priorities

Even the best scheduling is likely to be thrown off once reality comes rolling in with all its emergencies. It's worth putting some thought into how to best deal with that, and what parts of your schedule need and deserve extra protection.

What are your main challenges and danger zones? Which tasks are you most likely to neglect, or spend too much time on?

Where can you carve out more time for your most important tasks?

How can you protect that time?

Nourishment and Recovery

Taking enough guilt-free breaks is a serious challenge for many of us, but it is crucial if we want to give our best performance during our work hours.

The standard of a 40-hour workweek is not a coincidence; it is the tried and tested limit of human productivity over longer periods of time. When people try to work more, productivity actually goes down on the long run.

For mental work, such as working on a computer, the limit is even lower: estimates are that most people can perform well for a maximum 6 hours per day, but even less than that if the task requires a lot of focus, as is the case for tasks such as programming or creative writing.

You can think of this in two ways, whichever best fits your personality and helps you take your rest and recovery time seriously enough:

Think like an athlete:

Plan rest and nutrition into your training plan for optimal performance.

Or:

Think like a European:

Rediscover the art of taking breaks in order to achieve work-life balance and lead a fulfilled, productive, and joyful life.

Characteristics of a Great Break

So what does the ideal break look like? It depends, again, on the person and on the kind of task.

An ideal break should be:
- Rewarding
    - Something you look forward to
    - Something that has the power to motivate your work leading up to it

- Energizing
    - Bringing you back to work with more energy to get started again than when you left for the break, rather than less

- Relaxing
    - Helping you unwind if necessary
    - Easing physical tension and stress

- Nourishing (for body and soul)
    - Fuelling you for another stretch of uninterrupted and focused work
    - Satisfying your cravings
    - Fulfilling your needs for healthy nutrition

Types of Breaks

The best kinds of breaks fulfil as many as possible of those characteristics. Most breaks are combinations of the following:

1. Eating or Drinking

You probably already know how you need to eat in order to keep feeling good, energetic, and productive throughout the day. Very likely however (just statistically speaking…), the way you actually eat looks different from that.
Remember decision fatigue and construal levels: you will be much more likely to make good eating decisions if you plan your meals ahead of time, rather than decide what to eat for lunch once you're hungry.

Also, remember how glucose depletion affects decision-making, and vice versa. Make sure to plan enough healthy and satisfying meals and snacks to keep your brain fuelled. Also, if you can avoid making food decisions during the day, you'll have less decision fatigue and are keeping more of that precious will power for your actual tasks.

Planned meal breaks are also really great rewards that you can look forward to.

A special note for those who don't find healthy food rewarding:
- Many healthy foods are acquired tastes, so it's worth sticking to it for a while until you start to like it.
- Almost everything tastes surprisingly lovely if you're hungry and if there's nothing else around.
- For some healthy foods, it takes effort, creativity, skill and practice to turn them into something tasty without loading on too many calories. Ask yourself if it might be worth the investment to go that extra mile in order to get into healthier eating habits.

2. Working Out

Exercise can of course be physically exhausting, but for those of us who spend a lot of our work hours sitting at a desk, the right kind of workout can be very energizing and relaxing.

Is it rewarding though? Something to look forward to? Well, maybe not at first, but exercise is very much one of those things that gets more fun with more practice, and once the habits are strong enough. But it is worth finding the kind of exercise that has at least a potential to be rewarding eventually.

Not everybody has the same need for a lot of exercise in order to be happy — ask yourself what your own ideal amount and type of exercise would be and strive for that, not for anybody else's ideal.

3. Socializing

Meeting up with others can fun and energizing, and social breaks can very well be combined with eating or working out. Sometimes even work-related meetings can serve as a break.

For introverts however, social breaks can be draining, rather than energizing. Also, if you are working with people and your tasks are already very interactive, you may not want to spend your breaks around more people. So depending on your personality, but also on your work environment and tasks, you may want to avoid social breaks during the day, or you may want to plan for some additional alone time after a social break.

4. Disconnecting, Alone Time

Again, alone time can be combined with eating or working out, or it can be another form of escaping into your own world for a while, relaxing with a book or other entertainment.

What kinds of breaks work best for you?

What are some of the best ways for you to spend your biggest breaks (e.g., lunch break)?

What are some ways to spend shorter breaks in between smaller work units?

How can you make those smaller breaks rewarding?

What are things you want to do LESS during your breaks?

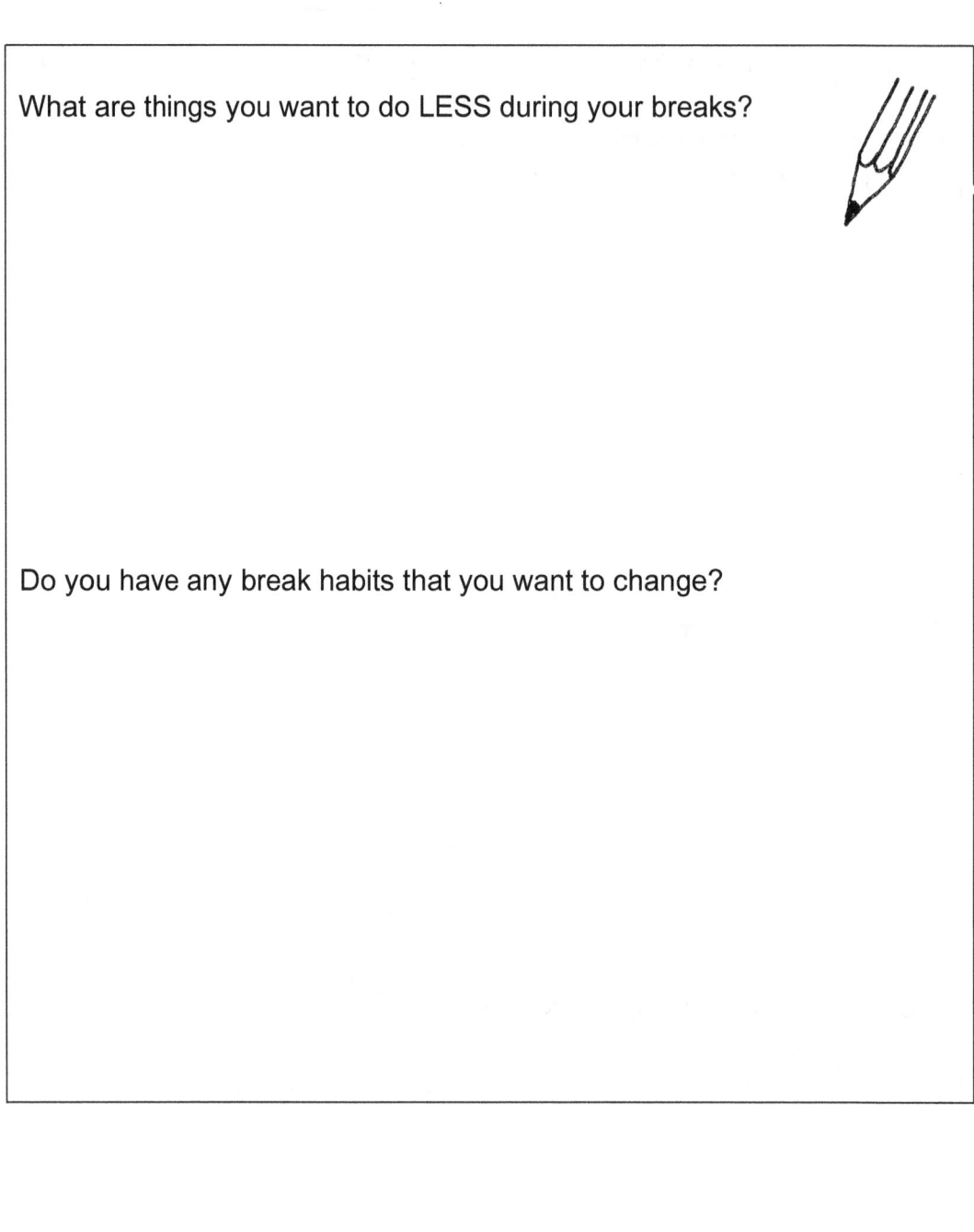

Do you have any break habits that you want to change?

To Summarize:

If you master the art of prioritizing and scheduling, including taking the right kinds of breaks, you will already make things much easier on your brain for several reasons. If you plan ahead of time, you will by thinking in a higher-level construal mode and making decisions that will benefit your future self most, rather than being guided by the momentary demands of your present self that seeks comfort and pleasure. Prioritizing and scheduling ahead of time also helps you reduce decision-fatigue, because you will not be making as many decisions throughout the day and can focus fully on the task. This means that you are already taking a big step towards reducing your switch costs.

In the following section, we will cover additional measures of how you can further improve your focus on the task and avoid switch costs wherever possible.

Focusing on One Task Only

So far, we have talked about the art of prioritizing and scheduling in healthy and realistic ways. Beyond having a well-planned schedule, how can you improve your work habits to reduce switch costs even more?

Based on what we know about the toll that task switching takes, our goal should be to reduce multi-tasking to the absolute minimum. For example, if you are updating a spreadsheet, you want to only update that spreadsheet. If you are writing an article, paper, or memo, you want to do nothing but write that article, paper, or memo. During that time, you want to only open websites that you need to access for that particular task. If you are checking email, you want to respond to every email you need to, and then quit the program and move on.

The following measures can make a big difference in allowing you that kind of focus.

- Unclutter your desktops — your actual outer workspace as well as your computer desktop.

- Quit applications the moment you stop using them, rather than leaving them open for later. The few seconds needed to restart the application later will be more than made up by your increased focus.

- Don't leave more browser windows open than necessary.

- Whenever you're on the Internet at all (whether you're doing research on an article or just going through email), you are likely to come across interesting links and articles that have the potential to distract you. Use something like InstaPaper for that. Instead of reading while you want to be working, simply click "read later" in the toolbar and close the tab. Whenever you have time to read, you go into InstaPaper (which you can do from a tablet or iphone) and read up on your saved stuff.

- Find a good system to answer your emails, in order to NOT spend time re-reading and re-considering emails without answering them. Follow the Inbox Zero principle (inboxzero.com) and only open your emails when you're ready to actually deal with them, rather than to just "check email". Then, deal with each new email very quickly, either by responding to it right away; by delegating (forwarding) it; by scheduling it for later; or by deleting or archiving it.

- Apply the Inbox Zero principle to your other tasks: if you find yourself thinking of something you need to do (or if you're getting a new assignment from somebody else), make it a habit to get the task out of your mind immediately by either getting it done right away, delegating it, scheduling it for later, or deciding not to do it.

- Put a system in place that helps you NOT think about tasks you're not currently doing. For example, use sticky notes, flash cards, or an app such as Evernote, as a temporary system for those moments when you need to write down something and don't have access to your calendar or list.

- Whatever system you use to organize your tasks, such as white board, graph paper, or online calendars, lists or notes: make sure that things don't get lost or overlap, and that you can synchronize easily across your different computers, mobile devices, and paper notes.

- To the extent that your job requirements allow it:
    - Turn off alerts and notifications wherever you can (phone, email, etc.).
    - Make a conscious choice at what times of the day you want to be social.
    - If necessary, let your co-workers or friends know that you're trying to cut back on distractions, and that you've scheduled specific time windows for your email response.
    - If you have a door that you can close, make a conscious choice when you want it open or closed.
    - If you work from home, physically separate your workspace from relaxation space.

- Play just as hard as you work: when you're on a break, focus on what you're doing, be present, rather than keeping half your brain at work. Not only will it clear your mind, but it also helps you hone your ability to focus. Think of being present as a skill and a habit that you want to practice everywhere.

What are your own biggest challenges with multitasking?

Which of the suggestions above apply to your own work and would be helpful to adopt?

How else could you reduce your multitasking?

Are there distractions that you will simply need to put up with, because they can't be avoided, or distractions that you choose to keep, because they are worth it?

Of all the things you could be improving, choose ONLY ONE that you want to try next:

Forming Habits

Building and Strengthening New Habits

Habits are very effective because, once established, they no longer require self-control. Also, thanks to the plasticity of our brains, even habits that are difficult to build at first do get easier over time, as new neural pathways form. After a while, the associations between one behavior and the next become automatic, rather than requiring constant effort and willpower.

Therefore, forming good habits is an excellent investment that will make things much easier down the road. The following strategies can help you build and strengthen new habits.

1. Set fixed times and get used to following that schedule.

For example, get into the habit of focusing on your most important task from 9:00 to 11:00 a.m. every weekday. After a while, you will get used to not checking emails during that time. Very likely, once you are used to that focused "zone" and have experienced it as rewarding, you will even start to crave that morning routine.

2. Find a way to integrate new habits into existing routines.

If you want to exercise more, find a way to integrate it into your commute, either by using the commute itself as a workout opportunity (by biking, walking, taking stairs), or by going to the gym on the way to or from work. Again, it may take a while, but it is likely that you will start craving that habit — if it is at all rewarding in some way. If it's not rewarding at all, on any level, maybe it's really not the right thing for you.

3. Set *action triggers* for yourself.

As an example, you could tell yourself "whenever I feel cold, before I put on a sweater, I'll do a set of pushups or jumping squats". In that case, "feeling cold" would serve as an action trigger for a quick workout.

Action triggers like these can be surprisingly effective in motivating action. One study looked at older patients who were recovering from hip or knee replacement surgery. Some of them were asked to set action triggers for their recovery exercises — something like, "I'll do my range-of-motion extensions every morning after I finish my first cup of coffee." The other group did not receive any coaching on action triggers. The results were dramatic: the patients who used action triggers recovered more than twice as fast, standing up on their own in three and a half weeks, instead of almost eight weeks for the others.

4. Change your environment to accommodate your new habit.

If you want to start eating more healthily, surround yourself only with healthy food, and with the right quantity of food. (This may sound obvious, but we all know it's not easy.)

Pick one...
Get started by deciding what specific new habit would be most important for you right now. *If a genie granted you the ability to adopt one specific new habit, what would that be?*

What changes in your schedule, routine and/or environment might promote that new habit?

What action trigger could you set for yourself to get started?

Changing Old Habits

If you want to change bad habits that are already strong, it helps to first figure out exactly what the habits consist of. Figure out your "habit loop":

1. What is the situation that triggers the habit?
2. What is your routine?
3. What is the reward that drives your behavior?

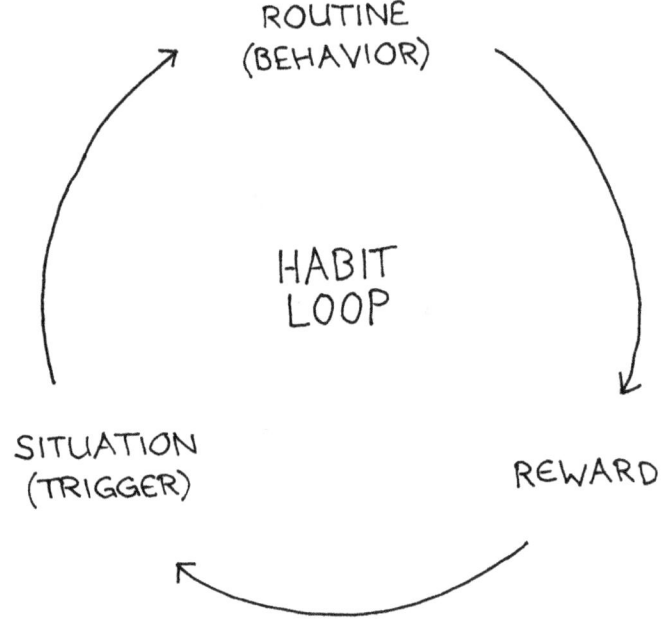

Once you've figured out your habit loop, the best way to change it is to find another reward that is as similar as possible, and figure out a new routine that would get you (almost) the same reward as the one that you are craving.

As an example: I have a habit of starting to watch a movie during a break, but then I get stuck and my break ends up taking more time than I intended. A way to keep that routine almost the same would be to watch a shorter video that has a similar entertainment and relaxation value, but with a predetermined length.

Another option is to avoid the situation that triggers your bad habit altogether. For example, I might want to avoid sitting down to watch videos during my break and go for a walk instead.

Draw a loop of one of your own habits that you would like to change.
- What's the situation (trigger)?
- What is your routine (behavior)?
- What is your reward?

BAD
HABIT
LOOP

Draw another loop. Where could you break out of your pattern most easily?
- Could you change the situation (avoid the trigger)?
- Or could you get the same reward with a healthier routine?
- If not, could you get at least a similar reward with a healthier routine?

Write your modifications into your new and improved habit loop, as suggestions for yourself. Do you want to give this new loop a try?

IMPROVED
HABIT
LOOP

Trouble Shooting

Frequent Problems

Estimating Time

Do you often have problems correctly estimating how long a task will take?

Suggestion A: Practice

Although of course life is never entirely predictable, time estimating is a skill that can be practiced.

If you want to get better at it, start tracking your tasks for a while. On your to-do list or calendar, write down how long you think each task will take before you start it. Then, when you do the task, time yourself and write down the actual time it took you to complete it.
Then, compare your estimates to the actual durations. Do you see a pattern? Are your estimates always off by the same percentage? Do your times vary dramatically, maybe depending on the time of day? Are there certain types of tasks you find harder to judge than others?

It is also possible that even though you correctly judge the task itself, you misjudge the transition time between different tasks (such as travel time, set-up time, clean-up time, etc.). In this case, logging and tracking can also help you figure out where you're off. Try tracking your entire day for a while, including breaks, meals and sleep, not just the tasks themselves.

Suggestion B: Buffers and Plans for Unexpected Time

Windows

Is your schedule often inherently unpredictable through no fault of your own? In that case you may want to not only plan in extra buffers (more than you think you need), but also find ways to be productive during unexpected openings. Have a plan, such as a special to-do list, for unexpected open times.

This is a good thing to have anyway, because oftentimes unexpected time windows—such as when somebody cancels a meeting, or when you're done with a task much faster than you think—go by unused because we have no plan for them.

Following Your Own Plans

Do you have a hard time following your own plans, even when you schedule realistically?

Suggestion

Something that can help is to "script" your behavior in more specific terms.

Psychologists call those plans *implementation intentions*. The idea is that we should not just form goal intentions ("I intend to achieve X"), but form implementation intentions instead ("I intend to perform specific goal-directed behavior Y when I encounter situation Z").

Goal intentions (more general)	**Implementation Intentions** (more specific)
	=> **if** situation, **then** behavior
e.g., "I want to promote our open house event."	e.g., "Today, right after coming back from lunch and before checking my messages, I will draft a press release, starting with the template of a previous event."

Note how this is a very similar concept to the action triggers we already talked about (p. 44).

Implementation intentions are particularly effective for two types of goals:

1. Goals that are associated with disagreeable tasks, such as phone calls or job applications.
2. Goals that are easily forgotten, such as taking medication.

These scripts are also particularly effective for people for whom realizing plans is especially difficult. For example, people suffering from depression, anxiety or addictions, seem to benefit greatly from this technique.

For many of your everyday tasks, a realistic schedule is already an implementation intention (e.g., "at 8am, I will sit down at my computer and start writing"). You may therefore not need to think about this technique often, because you are likely already doing it for many of your tasks. However, keep it in mind as a helpful technique for tasks that you find particularly difficult to get started with, or that you are likely to forget.

Form one implementation intention for a short-term goal, e.g., something you want to do this week:

If/when ...., I will ....

Form one implementation intention for a longer-term goal, e.g., something you want to do within the next three months:

If/when ...., I will ....

Procrastination

Although all the best practices we have covered here should already help you stick to your schedule, procrastination is a beast that deserves its own section.

Fun facts about procrastination:

- It is the number one reason for bad academic performance, according to students as well as teachers.
- It is the number one reason for health issues, according to doctors.
- It brings in an estimated $473 million extra tax revenues in the US annually, in form overpayments because of last minute rushing and errors.

To procrastinate means "to *voluntarily* delay an *intended* course of action *despite expecting to be worse off for the delay*".

Note that procrastination is not simply the inability to do a task because of an overloaded schedule, or because of interruptions or external constraints. It is a *voluntary* delay.

But the second part of the definition is also crucial: if we're procrastinating, we do it despite our better knowledge, fully *expecting to be worse off later*. Procrastination is not a productive way of delaying a task — those certainly exist, but they don't fall under the term "procrastination". Also, procrastination is not a healthy form of relaxation or even simply laziness - procrastinators feel bad about their decisions to delay and don't usually enjoy their "time off".

> Procrastination is a *gap between intention and action*.

What about the claim that procrastination improves performance, because the imminent deadline creates excitement and pressure that elicit peak performance ("I do my best work under pressure")? Research suggests this is unlikely: in one study, self-proclaimed procrastinators actually performed worse under pressure than non-procrastinators.
Or what about the possibility that the stress and illness caused by procrastination might be offset by the enjoyment of carefree times earlier?

That, too, does not seem to be the case. In one study, procrastinating students reported lower stress and less illness than non-procrastinators early in the semester, but they reported higher stress and more illness later in the term, were overall sicker, and received lower grades.

In other words, procrastination really does seem to be a self-defeating behavior pattern, marked by some short-term benefits, but larger long-term costs.

What are your own procrastination traps?

What kinds of tasks are you most likely to delay, even though you want to get them done?

Do you know why that is the case? What is holding you up?

How are you most likely to procrastinate? (What do you do instead of your intended task?)

Suggestion A: Awareness of Costs and Benefits

Usually, for anything we do voluntarily, there are not only costs but also benefits. **What are the costs, but also the benefits, of your own procrastination?**

Benefits of Procrastinating:	Costs of Procrastinating:

Giving the benefits of procrastination some conscious thought can help you decide whether you're ready to give them up. It may also help you figure out other ways to get similar benefits.

Suggestion B: Divide and Conquer

If you're "not in the mood", just do 15 minutes of something. Just get started. Then take a break - not in the other order... Remember that it's a lot better to work just 15 minutes on something than not at all.

The more resistance you have, the more you need to plan ahead, make the work increments small enough, and make the rewards attractive enough. Go easy with the plan, put in buffers, but stick to the core elements of your schedule (including your breaks).

> **Rule of thumb:**
>
> If you have a hard time getting started or keeping focused:
> - Try smaller work units.
> - Try longer and better rest or reward periods.

Suggestion C: Keep Reading

Since there are so many different reasons for people to procrastinate, there are also many different ways to beat it. The DIY tool-kit in the next chapter was originally developed as an intervention to help people beat procrastination. It is a two-step intervention program that will help you assess yourself, diagnose your problems, and optimize your own work habits.

DIY Repair: Toolkit For Your Own Assessment and Interventions

The best way to optimize your own work habits is to do your own assessment and design your own interventions. This last part of the workbook will give you a toolkit to do just that.

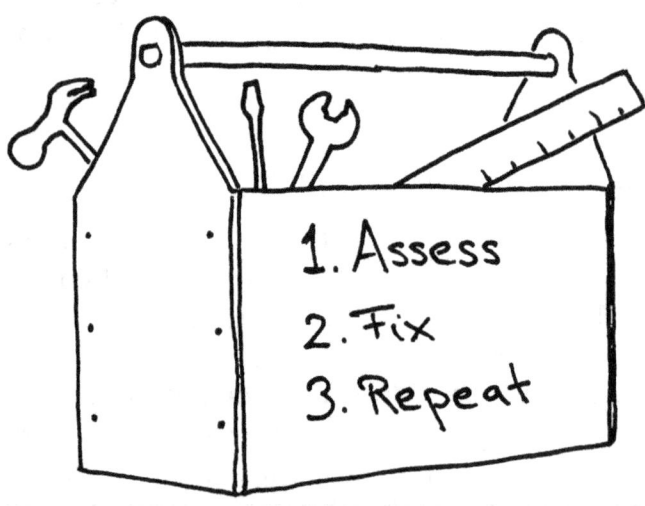

1. Assessment: Diagnosing the Problem

The first step in this intervention is to become more aware of what your obstacles are.

Every person is different!

To find that out, **keep a productivity log**. You'll find a template on the next pages as well as at the end of the workbook. You can also download a printable pdf of the template for your own use here: http://www.teuscher-counseling.com/resources/.

Here is how it works: the night before your workday, write a to-do list and a schedule for the following day. Make sure to schedule realistically, in your optimal time units as discussed above, include breaks, etc. Next to the planned schedule, have an empty column. As your workday unfolds, write into the empty column what you actually did.

—Warning: this may be painful!—

Throughout that day, take notes of what happened when you did or didn't stay on track. If there were no outside interruptions, what were your thoughts when you did something other than what you intended?

Keep this log for at least several days (more is better, but they don't need to be consecutive days), then start analyzing patterns. Are there things that repeatedly trip you up?

Planned Day		Actual Day	
Time	Activity (To Do)	Time	Activity (Did)

Notes
What happened? What were obstacles, reasons for deviating from the plan? What were successes?

Another way to assess your current work habits is to take a look at your past:

What were times in your life when you were most productive?

What was different then? What was fostering that productivity?

Were there also times when you were less productive than you are now?

What was different then, and how can you avoid those situations?

Examples of Problems and Obstacles You May Find

Here is a list of the problems that I've encountered most frequently in my coaching experience (and in myself). The examples may help you get more clarity about your own reasons for not sticking to your schedule or being otherwise unhappy about your productivity.

Fear

This could be fear of the task itself, or it could be fear of the consequences of doing the task. For example, you might feel anxious about making a phone call simply because you don't like talking on the phone, or you might be anxious because the phone call could result in failure or disappointment.

If your task is to give a presentation, you could be afraid that your audience will be critical of it. You might want to write a book, but worry that you won't be able to sell it. You might want to apply for a job, but worry about not getting it — or about getting it but then hating it or not being good at it. All those fears can distract you from your task or keep you from even getting started.

Lack of skills or knowledge to do the task

You may simply not know how to do the task, or lack the skills to do it efficiently.

Uncertainty or confusion

Not having a clear plan of what you need to do next is a very common hold-up. This uncertainty can lead to a vague feeling of being overwhelmed, even if you do have the necessary skills and are not afraid of the task. This is frequently a problem for bigger projects.

Lack of purpose or passion

You may have doubts about whether you're on the right track at all, or be uncertain whether your work will lead to long-term success.

Resentment

The recurring thought "I shouldn't have to do this" can make it hard to execute tasks others have assigned us, particularly when we think they are unnecessary (excessive paperwork) or unfair (fixing a problem that someone else made).

Resentment can infuse our entire work life if we feel that a past injustice—losing a previous job, not getting a promotion we'd been told to expect—led to taking the job in the first place.

Exhaustion

Having worked for too long on a task can make you lose your focus.

Hunger, thirst or cravings

Either actual hunger or thirst, or just cravings, can be reasons (or excuses) for leaving the desk.

Lack of urgency or accountability

Too much freedom with a task can be a problem, in particular a lack of accountability or supervision, or deadlines that are too far away.

Truly disagreeable or painful task

This might seem the most obvious obstacle, but it is surprisingly rare in my experience as a reason for procrastination. Truly disagreeable tasks could for example be:
- physically painful
- excruciatingly boring
- humiliating

Interruptions

Outside interruptions such as phone calls or people stepping into your office can be legitimate reasons for not sticking to your plans – they may or may not be avoidable, depending on your work.

Addictive distractions or entertainment

Games, TV series, social media or other kinds of Internet browsing can have addictive qualities and can take up tremendous amounts of time. People are often reluctant to admit even to themselves just how much time they spend with these activities, and logging those hours requires a good amount of courage to face an unpleasant truth.

Distracting Thoughts

Being distracted by our own thoughts is a frequent reason to lose focus, whether we're simply daydreaming, or planning dinner, or adding items to a mental shopping list.

Other tasks than the one you really wanted to do

You may find that you often do other tasks than the one you intended, for example because the previous tasks take longer than anticipated, or because you're held up by unexpected problems.
For example, you may find that you write emails during the time you wanted to do something else. If you work from home, you may suddenly find yourself doing chores rather than doing the work you intended.

Inertia

Sometimes we simply have troubles getting out of bed or off the couch. This can be a particular problem for people who have lower energy to begin with, or who have a tendency toward depression.
Inertia is often problem in the morning, when people have a hard time getting up at the time they wanted (especially those with freedom over their own schedule, who don't need to be at work at a specific time). During the day, inertia can also lead to breaks that go on for much longer than intended.

Fun activities

There are always other things that are simply more fun than the task you should be doing. They could either pull you away from your task, or, more likely, keep you away from it in the first place.
What often happens is that we start doing something fun during a break, and then keep doing it longer than we intended. Social interactions in particular often take more time than expected.

2. Treatment: Designing an Intervention

Once you have figured out what is tripping you up, create a specific intervention. Target only one problem at a time. See it as an experiment that you do with yourself. Whatever you try, do it for at least one week.

If you like the change, stick to it for another two weeks, even if it's hard, because it takes a while for habits to form. By that time you will likely find it easier and will be able to keep the new habit, if it is making a positive difference in your life.

Examples of Solutions (but you'll need to find your own!)

If the trigger is fear

- Divide and conquer:
    - Start with the easiest part.
    - Or start with the scariest part.
- Don't aim for perfection.
- Acknowledge the fear – it's ok to be afraid, it doesn't mean we can't act.
- Think of your fear as "excitement" – they feel very similar and are often both appropriate.
- Do one scary thing per day (e.g., make a daily checklist for little scary things to get done every day).

If the problem is lack of skills or knowledge to do the task

- Get training.
- Delegate.
- Ask for help.

If the problem is uncertainty or confusion

- Write a very specific list as a way of finding out what needs to be done.
- Schedule "figuring out what needs to be done next" as if it were the actual task – because it is.

If you're lacking a purpose or passion to keep you motivated

- Reconnect with your values: why are doing what you're doing?
- Are you on the right track?

- o If not, explore alternatives.
- o Or do you have good reasons to stay on the wrong track? If so, it IS the right track. Own it.
- Find a way to increase your skills – becoming better at what we're doing often leads to more passion.

If the problem is resentment

- Recognize it.
- Decide how much room you want to give it.
- Sometimes, the decision to "grow up and get over it" actually works.
- Sometimes, a ritual of grieving or forgiveness can help people deal with past injustices.

If you're simply too exhausted

- Take more breaks.
- Take longer breaks.
- Take better breaks (see p. 26).

If hunger, thirst or cravings are impairing your work

- Re-think your eating habits.
- Recognize which cravings you don't need to give in to.
- Find a replacement reward for the cravings (see p.36).

If the problem is lack of urgency or accountability from deadlines that are too far away

- Set earlier deadlines for partial achievements.
- Make them real by scheduling rewards: plan something fun for the end of the project.
- If you have a supervisor, talk about your goals and make commitments.
- Get accountability by promising somebody results at different stages of a project.
- Announce your commitments to friends or colleagues.
- Find a partner to work with and check in on a regular basis.
- Get an accountability buddy.
- Get a coach.

If the task is truly disagreeable, boring, or otherwise painful

- Try to make it more attractive by turning it into a game, listening to music, getting company.
- Cut it into shorter units.
- Find better rewards.

If you get a lot of outside interruptions

- Shield yourself better by disconnecting and closing doors.
- If the interruptions are necessary, recognize that and schedule accordingly.

If you're wasting a lot of time with addictive distractions or entertainment

- Reduce temptation: restrict access to certain websites to certain times.
- Use a separate device (or separate computer accounts) for working than for games or entertainment.
- Set yourself a weekly or daily time limit for TV, movies, games etc.
- Set up realistic rules, such as "no games before 5pm".
- As more radical approaches: block certain websites entirely, get rid of games, get rid of the TV, and go back to the newspaper for news.

If you're distracted by your own thoughts

- Start meditating to increase your ability to focus.
- If your daydreaming is pleasant, take breaks that are specifically dedicated to that.
- If your distracting thoughts are practical and useful (planning, thinking about things you need to do later), write them down to get them out of your head.

If the problem is spending too much time on other tasks

- Re-think your schedule: was it realistic?
- Can you delegate?
- Are there task you could have avoided?
- Implement the "Inbox Zero" principle (p. 40) for your emails, but also for other smaller tasks that may come up during the day.

If the problem is that you never get started (inertia)

- Get up one hour earlier, do one work unit (small task, or 30 min) before breakfast. Try for at least one entire week.

If the problem is that the distractions are too much fun

- Use them as rewards.
- Plan your social interactions at times of the day when you're least productive anyway. For most people, that is later in the day.

3. Rinse and Repeat: Experimenting and Tweaking

Remember that this is an experimental approach. Whatever you try, look at it as an experiment that may succeed or fail. Either way, you learned something important that will help you fine-tune your work habits. After going through Step 1 (Assessment) and Step 2 (Treatment; Intervention), you will likely observe some changes. If you don't like them, or if you feel that there could be even more improvement, repeat both steps. If your assessment in Step 1 gave you a lot to work with, you may only need to repeat Step 2 by trying a new intervention, or by tweaking what you tried before in order to make it work even better.

Also, remember that it takes a lot of practice to become an expert at anything difficult. Managing our time well is an inherently difficult skill, so be patient with yourself and don't give up if things don't improve right away. Take on your next obstacle and try the next intervention.

It is also a good idea to do the entire two-step intervention with other people, for example with a friend, in a group, or with a coach. Not only does this give you accountability, which makes a huge difference, but it also adds more creative power to the process. When other people are helping you think, it will be much easier to diagnose your triggers and find new solutions that work for you.

Productivity Journal: Template For Your Own Use

The following pages will get you through a week of journaling. After that, you can download a printable template for the Productivity Journal from my website:
http://www.teuscher-counseling.com/resources/

Planned Day		Actual Day	
Time	Activity (To Do)	Time	Activity (Did)

Notes
What happened? What were obstacles, reasons for deviating from the plan? What were successes?

Planned Day		Actual Day	
Time	Activity (To Do)	Time	Activity (Did)

Notes
What happened? What were obstacles, reasons for deviating from the plan? What were successes?

Planned Day		Actual Day	
Time	Activity (To Do)	Time	Activity (Did)

Notes
What happened? What were obstacles, reasons for deviating from the plan? What were successes?

Planned Day		Actual Day	
Time	Activity (To Do)	Time	Activity (Did)

Notes
What happened? What were obstacles, reasons for deviating from the plan? What were successes?

Planned Day		Actual Day	
Time	Activity (To Do)	Time	Activity (Did)

Notes
What happened? What were obstacles, reasons for deviating from the plan? What were successes?

Planned Day		Actual Day	
Time	Activity (To Do)	Time	Activity (Did)

Notes
What happened? What were obstacles, reasons for deviating from the plan? What were successes?

Planned Day		Actual Day	
Time	Activity (To Do)	Time	Activity (Did)

Notes
What happened? What were obstacles, reasons for deviating from the plan? What were successes?

References

Arrington, C. M., & Logan, G. D. (2004). The Cost of a Voluntary Task Switch. *Psychological Science, 15*(9), 610–615.

American Psychological Association (2006). Multitasking: Switching costs. *http://www.apa.org*. Retrieved December 15, 2013, from http://www.apa.org/research/action/multitask.aspx

Baumeister, R. F. (2002). Ego Depletion and Self-Control Failure: An Energy Model of the Self's Executive Function. Self and Identity, 1(2), 129-136.

Baumeister, R. F., Heatherton, T. F., & Tice, D. M. (1994). *Losing control: How and why people fail at self-regulation*. San Diego: Academic Press.

Bechtold, S. E., Janaro, R. E., & Sumners, D. W. L. (1984). Maximization of Labor Productivity Through Optimal Rest-Break Schedules. *Management Science, 30* (12), 1442-1458.

Boksem, M. A. S., Meijman, T. F., & Lorist, M. M. (2005). Effects of mental fatigue on attention: An ERP study. *Cognitive Brain Research, 25*(1), 107-116.

Cameron, J. (1992). The Artist's Way: A Spiritual Path to Higher Creativity (1st ed.). Tarcher.

Covey, S. R., Merrill, A. R., & Merrill, R. R. (1996). *First things first: to live, to love, to learn, to leave a legacy*. Simon and Schuster.

Crenshaw, D. (2008). *The myth of multitasking: how doing it all gets nothing done*. San Francisco: Jossey-Bass.

Danziger, S., Levav, J., & Avnaim-Pesso, L. (2011). Extraneous factors in judicial decisions. *Proceedings of the National Academy of Sciences, 108*(17), 6889–6892.

De Jonge, J., Spoor, E., Sonnentag, S., Dormann, C., & van den Tooren, M. (2012). "Take a break?!" Off-job recovery, job demands, and job resources as predictors of health, active learning, and creativity. *European Journal of Work and Organizational Psychology*, 21(3), 321–348.

Duhigg, Ch. (2012). *The power of habit: why we do what we do in life and business.* Random House.

Ferrari, J. R. (2001). Procrastination as self-regulation failure of performance: effects of cognitive load, self-awareness, and time limits on 'working best under pressure'." *European Journal of Personality, 15*, 391–406.

Fuster, J. M. (1988). Prefrontal Cortex. In *Comparative Neuroscience and Neurobiology* (pp. 107–109). Birkhäuser Boston.

Fuster, J. M. (2001). The Prefrontal Cortex-An Update - Time Is of the Essence. *Neuron, 30*(2), 319–333.

Gailliot, M. T., Baumeister, R. F., Nathan, C., Maner, J. K., Ashby, E., Tice, D. M., Brewer, L. E., & Schmeichel, B. J. (2007). Self-control relies on glucose as a limited energy source: Willpower is more than a metaphor. *Journal of Personality and Social Psychology, 92*(2), 325–336.

Gailliot, M. T., & Baumeister, R. F. (2007). The Physiology of Willpower: Linking Blood Glucose to Self-Control. *Personality and Social Psychology Review, 11*(4), 303–327.

Gladwell, M. (2011). *Outliers: The Story of Success.* Little, Brown and Company.

Godin, S. (2011). *Linchpin: Are You Indispensable?* Portfolio Trade. Retrieved from http://www.amazon.ca/exec/obidos/redirect?tag=citeulike09-20&path=ASIN/1591844096

Gollwitzer, P. M. (1999). Implementation intentions: Strong effects of simple plans. *American Psychologist, 54* (7), 493–503.

Gollwitzer, P. M., & Brandstätter, V. (1997). Implementation intentions and effective goal pursuit. *Journal of Personality and Social Psychology, 73* (1), 186–199.

Hagger, M. S.; Wood, C.; Stiff, C.; Chatzisarantis, N. L. D. (2010). Ego Depletion and the Strength Model of Self-Control: A Meta-Analysis. *Psychological Bulletin, 136* (4), 495–525.

Heath, Ch. and Heath, D. (2010). *Switch: how to change things when change is hard*. Random House.

Henning, R. A., Jacques, P., Kissel, G. V., Sullivan, A. B., & Alteras-Webb, S. M. (1997). Frequent short rest breaks from computer work: effects on productivity and well-being at two field sites. *Ergonomics, 40*(1), 78–91.

Hofstadter, Douglas R. (1999) [1979] *Gödel, Escher, Bach: An Eternal Golden Braid*. Basic Books.

Jansen, N. W. H., Kant, Ij., & Brandt, P. A. van den. (2002). Need for recovery in the working population: Description and associations with fatigue and psychological distress. *International Journal of Behavioral Medicine, 9*(4), 322–340.

Jones, E.E., & Berglas, S.C. (1978). Control of attributions about the self through self handicapping strategies: The appeal of alcohol and the role of underachievement. *Personality and Social Psychology Bulletin, 4*, 200-206.

Kahneman, Daniel; Tversky, Amos (1979). "Intuitive prediction: biases and corrective procedures". *TIMS Studies in Management Science, 12*, 313–327.

Landrigan, C. P., Rothschild, J. M., Cronin, J. W., Kaushal, R., Burdick, E., Katz, J. T., ... Czeisler, C. A. (2004). Effect of Reducing Interns' Work Hours on Serious Medical Errors in Intensive Care Units. *New England Journal of Medicine, 351* (18), 1838–1848.

Lieberman, H. R. (2003). Nutrition, brain function and cognitive performance. *Appetite, 40* (3), 245–254.

Liberman, N., & Trope, Y. (1998). The role of feasibility and desirability considerations in near and distant future decisions: A test of temporal construal theory. *Journal of Personality and Social Psychology, 75* (1), 5–18.

Liberman, N., Sagristano, M. D., & Trope, Y. (2002). The effect of temporal distance on level of mental construal. *Journal of Experimental Social Psychology, 38* (6), 523–534.

Lim, J., Wu, W., Wang, J., Detre, J. A., Dinges, D. F., & Rao, H. (2010). Imaging brain fatigue from sustained mental workload: An ASL perfusion study of the time-on-task effect. *NeuroImage, 49* (4), 3426–3435.

Loewenstein, G., Read, D., & Baumeister, R. F. (2003). *Time and Decision: Economic and Psychological Perspectives on Intertemporal Choice.* Russell Sage Foundation.

Mann, M. (2012): http://inboxzero.com.

Might, M. (2012): Boost your productivity: Cripple your technology. http://matt.might.net/articles/cripple-your-technology/

Monsell, S. (2003). Task switching. *Trends in Cognitive Sciences, 7*(3), 134–140.

Robinson, S (2012). Why We Have to Go Back to a 40-Hour Work Week to Keep Our Sanity. http://www.alternet.org/visions/154518/why_we_have_to_go_back_to_a_40-hour_work_week_to_keep_our_sanity?page=entire

Rock, D. (2009). *Your brain at work: strategies for overcoming distraction, regaining focus, and working smarter all day long.* [New York]: Harper Business.

Silvia, P. J. (2007). *How to Write a Lot: A Practical Guide to Productive Academic Writing.* American Psychological Association.

Steel, P. (2007). The nature of procrastination: a meta-analytic and theoretical review of quintessential self-regulatory failure. *Psychological Bulletin, 133* (1), 65–94.

Teuscher, U., & Mitchell, S. (2011). Relation Between Time Perspective and Delay Discounting: A Literature Review. *The Psychological Record, 61*(4).

Tice, D. M., & Baumeister, R. F. (1997). Longitudinal Study of Procrastination, Performance, Stress, and Health: The Costs and Benefits of Dawdling. *Psychological Science, 8* (6), 454–458.

Tracy, B. (2007). *Eat that frog!: 21 great ways to stop procrastinating and get more done in less time.* San Francisco, CA: Berrett-Koehler Publishers.

Trope, Y., & Liberman, N. (2000). Temporal construal and time-dependent changes in preference. *Journal of Personality and Social Psychology, 79* (6), 876–889.

Van Veldhoven, M., & Broersen, S. (2003). Measurement quality and validity of the "need for recovery scale." *Occupational and Environmental Medicine, 60,* 3-9.

Vohs, K. D., Baumeister, R. F., Schmeichel, B. J., Twenge, J. M., Nelson, N. M., & Tice, D. M. (2008). Making choices impairs subsequent self-control: A limited-resource account of decision making, self-regulation, and active initiative. *Journal of Personality and Social Psychology, 94* (5), 883–898.

Liberman, N., Sagristano, M. D., & Trope, Y. (2002). The effect of temporal distance on level of mental construal. *Journal of Experimental Social Psychology, 38* (6), 523–534.

Lim, J., Wu, W., Wang, J., Detre, J. A., Dinges, D. F., & Rao, H. (2010). Imaging brain fatigue from sustained mental workload: An ASL perfusion study of the time-on-task effect. *NeuroImage, 49* (4), 3426–3435.

Loewenstein, G., Read, D., & Baumeister, R. F. (2003). *Time and Decision: Economic and Psychological Perspectives on Intertemporal Choice.* Russell Sage Foundation.

Mann, M. (2012): http://inboxzero.com.

Might, M. (2012): Boost your productivity: Cripple your technology. http://matt.might.net/articles/cripple-your-technology/

Monsell, S. (2003). Task switching. *Trends in Cognitive Sciences, 7*(3), 134–140.

Robinson, S (2012). Why We Have to Go Back to a 40-Hour Work Week to Keep Our Sanity. http://www.alternet.org/visions/154518/why_we_have_to_go_back_to_a_40-hour_work_week_to_keep_our_sanity?page=entire

Rock, D. (2009). *Your brain at work: strategies for overcoming distraction, regaining focus, and working smarter all day long.* [New York]: Harper Business.

Silvia, P. J. (2007). *How to Write a Lot: A Practical Guide to Productive Academic Writing.* American Psychological Association.

Steel, P. (2007). The nature of procrastination: a meta-analytic and theoretical review of quintessential self-regulatory failure. *Psychological Bulletin, 133* (1), 65–94.

Teuscher, U., & Mitchell, S. (2011). Relation Between Time Perspective and Delay Discounting: A Literature Review. *The Psychological Record, 61*(4).

Tice, D. M., & Baumeister, R. F. (1997). Longitudinal Study of Procrastination, Performance, Stress, and Health: The Costs and Benefits of Dawdling. *Psychological Science, 8* (6), 454–458.

Tracy, B. (2007). *Eat that frog!: 21 great ways to stop procrastinating and get more done in less time*. San Francisco, CA: Berrett-Koehler Publishers.

Trope, Y., & Liberman, N. (2000). Temporal construal and time-dependent changes in preference. *Journal of Personality and Social Psychology, 79* (6), 876–889.

Van Veldhoven, M., & Broersen, S. (2003). Measurement quality and validity of the "need for recovery scale." *Occupational and Environmental Medicine, 60*, 3-9.

Vohs, K. D., Baumeister, R. F., Schmeichel, B. J., Twenge, J. M., Nelson, N. M., & Tice, D. M. (2008). Making choices impairs subsequent self-control: A limited-resource account of decision making, self-regulation, and active initiative. *Journal of Personality and Social Psychology, 94* (5), 883–898.

More About This Topic

Free Monthly Newsletter
Creative Decision Making and Goal Achievement
by Ursina Teuscher, PhD

Sign up here:
http://www.teuscher-counseling.com/blog

This free newsletter will bring you updates on new research findings; featured videos or articles; Ursina's personal book recommendations (fiction as well as non-fiction); and announcements of special events. It covers topics around decision-making, creative and rational thinking, goal achievement, procrastination, time management, coaching, etc.

Coaching Group Programs or Individual Coaching
by Ursina Teuscher, PhD

Sign up for a group coaching program here:
http://www.teuscher-counseling.com/procrastination

Get more information on my website or by contacting me directly:
http://www.teuscher-counseling.com

About the Author

Ursina Teuscher has a PhD in psychology and a professional degree (MS) as a career counselor from the University of Freiburg, Switzerland. As a decision coach and consultant, she helps individuals and organizations think more creatively and systematically about their decisions, and achieve their goals.

Ursina's published research and teaching over the years has focused on cognitive psychology and neuroscience, learning, memory, decision making, and coaching techniques. Her consulting and educational projects include strategic planning for small businesses and non-profit organizations, and post-graduate training courses in decision aiding techniques for career counselors.

She currently teaches decision making classes at Portland State University (PSU) and at the Small Business Development Center at Portland Community College (CLIMB PCC).

http://www.teuscher-counseling.com

www.ingramcontent.com/pod-product-compliance
Lightning Source LLC
Chambersburg PA
CBHW081732170526
45167CB00009B/3797